D1395429

The
Fireside
Book
2020

"There's not a word yet for old friends who've just met."
— Jim Henson

Contents

Poetry

From The Manse Window

Nature's Calendar

Illustrations by Sarah Holliday and Mandy Dixon.

Happy New Year!

Some say that time's a river,
A calm and steady flow,
I guess that's one perception,
But me – I just don't know.

I'm sure when I was younger,
Time never seemed to race
Each New Year came decades apart
They crept so slow a pace.

Yet now they seem to come each week,
And birthdays just as quick,
I wish that Time would just slow down,
It goes at such a lick!

So if you seek a moral here,
I think I'd simply say
Enjoy each moment of this year,
And savour every day.

Maggie Ingall.

An Unexpected Spring

I draw back the January curtains
Expecting darkness and gloom,
Instead, a dazzling sight meets my eyes –
The garden has burst into bloom.

The branches are gently bending
And clothed in new buds of snow,
The garrya's catkins have vanished –
Now tassels of icicles grow.

The faded lawn's so bright and gleaming
And as pristine as a new day,
The hawthorn is covered in blossom
Much whiter than any in May.

It looks like a garden makeover team
Crept in and worked all through the night,
Transforming my dark winter garden
To a world full of sparkle and light.

Eliza Barret.

Hygge Happiness

Our Harry's into *hygge*; it's from Denmark, by the way,
It's simple things like cosy nights and friends coming to stay.
It's all about contentment. And what makes you feel good,
Like hot sweet drinks on winter nights and favourite comfort food.

They're also big on blankets, for snuggling, if you please,
You pile them high and hug them close to keep away the freeze.
The Danes are into candles; their nights are dark and long,
Log fires, too, are *hyggeligt* – my *hygge* sense burns strong!

We all should find our cosy. Our hug. Our happy place.
For things like phones and cash and cars won't help you find head space.
So snuggle in your blanket, and drink your warming brew,
And remember – if the Danes can master comfort, so can you!

Judy Jarvie.

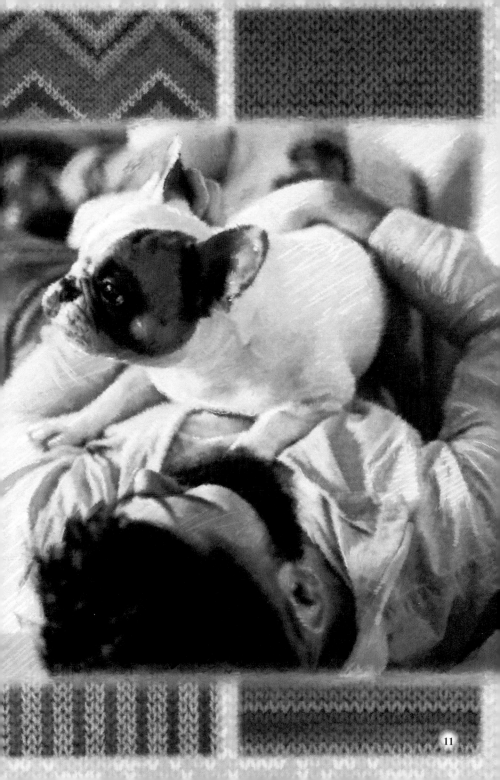

Signs

Though days remain short and the weather still cold
There are signs that the winter is losing its hold.
The sun's rays spread further and so does the thaw,
And birds seem more vocal than they've been before.

And in sheltered corners a flower may appear,
Welcome portent of the spring, a gallant pioneer.
And its cheering presence can serve to remind us
That winter's dark days can soon be put behind us.

J. Darley.

Many Happy Returns!

Today's my birthday, fancy that,
The birthday cards dropped on the mat
Are open now, and on display,
And do you know what they all say?
A certain person, namely me,
Is sixty now! That cannot be!
I feel that life has just begun,
It's full of laughter, full of fun,
In fact, it's great to be alive,
And in my head I'm twenty-five!

Linda Brown.

from the Manse Window

Incredible Moments

MANY years ago some friends bought me a book of extracts from the gospels illustrated by paintings from Jesus's life by the artist Angus McBride.

Jesus is depicted as a strong young man, obviously Jewish, with dark curly hair and beard, rather than the westernised image so often presented to us with pale skin, blue eyes and long hair and a rather effeminate aura.

One of my favourite pictures is of Jesus and his disciples seated around a camp fire on top of a mountain at the end of the day as the purple and blue shadows gather.

I imagine I'm part of the group, resting, chatting, eating, discussing the amazing things they've probably seen that day. I wonder how often they stopped to reflect on where they'd come from and where they were at that moment.

Did they ever ask the question, "How did this happen to me?"

There were so many incredible moments. In Matthew's gospel,

two events follow each other in quick succession.

The first was the feeding of the 5,000, when not only did Jesus demonstrate his power over the physical world by making something out of very little, but there was also a surplus. Did they shake their heads in wonder and disbelief as they gathered it up?

That is followed by the weird experience of being without Jesus on a boat on the lake at midnight when they see him walking towards them on the water.

They think they're seeing a ghost, and even when Jesus assures them that it's him they're not convinced. Peter says, "If it's really you, then command me to walk on the water."

I can imagine the rest of them thinking: "What, Peter, are you mad? This is crazy enough as it is!" Then Peter gets out of the boat and begins to walk on the water.

These stories are so familiar to us that we just accept them, but put yourself in the place of these men. What would they ▶

iStock.

by Rev. Susan Sarapuk.

16

▶ have felt? They were dealing with mind-blowing events every day which must have been overwhelming. Did they ever long for the old life when everything was quiet and predictable?

There was a return to that, of sorts, after Jesus's death and resurrection. Some of them went back to fishing because it was the anchor, the safe place they were used to before all of this incredible stuff started happening.

But when Jesus appeared on the seashore they knew then that there would be no going back.

To follow Jesus is a challenge. It can be unsettling and often frightening when we deal with stuff which is new and stretches us. That doesn't mean we should retreat to what is predictable and ordinary.

Peter was the one who actually got out of the boat and started walking on the water. He was probably as confused and alarmed as the others, but he was determined to prove whether Jesus was real or just a ghost. He was moving forward.

He was also the first to declare his belief that Jesus was the Messiah, and he was the only one who followed the soldiers to the house of the high priest after Jesus was arrested.

All these things were challenging and frightening, but he kept pressing ahead because he wanted to follow Jesus no matter what.

He'd had a taste of a different life and he wanted more. He knew he was never going back to the predictable and the ordinary. God had taken hold of him.

There's a moment in the gospels when some of Jesus's followers turn back because of the things he's saying. Jesus looks at the twelve disciples and asks if they're going to leave him, too, and elicits the response: "Where would we go, Lord? You have the words of life."

People look for meaning and purpose in life. Young people want experiences; they want to travel the world, have money, success, fame, and they want to put it all on Instagram to declare to everyone else that they're having a wonderful time and that their life is exciting, and more exciting than the next person's.

Wisdom comes with age, when we come to understand that it's the simple things that matter – love, family, friends, a place to belong – but that doesn't mean that life should be ordinary and predictable.

The greatest challenge and joy in life, no matter what stage we're at, is to be a disciple of Jesus, to keep learning new things every day as we walk by faith.

Many people imagine Christianity to be boring – you go to church on a Sunday and sing some dry hymns and then you try to live a good life the rest of the time.

It was the same in Jesus's day. You go to the synagogue on the Sabbath and you try to keep the commandments and obey the law. But when Jesus came along he brought spiritual reality into spiritual rules.

He taught his disciples that religion wasn't about paying lip service – it was about knowing and experiencing the power of God.

The lives of his followers were turned upside down. They would never go back to what they were before.

Being with Jesus was exhilarating and joyous, but also confusing and unsettling.

It's the same for anyone who wants to be a disciple. There will be times of great joy and discovery, but also times of pain and confusion when we will want to walk away. It's in those times that God is really stretching us, teaching us new things and changing us.

Would you really want to go back? What is there to go back to when you have experienced Life? Think of yourself sitting around that camp fire on the mountain with Jesus. You're safe with him. Relax. ∎

Nature's Calendar For Spring

March is Dolphin Awareness Month. Did you know dolphins can send just one half of their brain to sleep at a time? It helps them stay alert to threats.

Rhubarb can be at its best around now. The fruit experienced a boom between the two world wars, as the price of sugar dropped and made eating it a lot more palatable and popular.

The dry season is beginning now in Borneo. The country has an unspoiled wilderness that's perfect for visiting, with 140 million acres of rainforest.

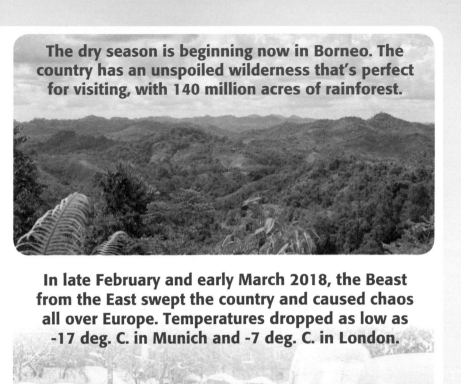

In late February and early March 2018, the Beast from the East swept the country and caused chaos all over Europe. Temperatures dropped as low as -17 deg. C. in Munich and -7 deg. C. in London.

St Patrick, Ireland's patron saint, was originally associated with the colour blue. It wasn't until the day was connected with the Irish independence movement in the late 18th century that green became the official colour of the day.

To A Snowdrop

A flash of white, a hint of green,
Where barren earth before had been.
You quietly steal upon the scene,
Demure and coy,
A springtime herald, gladly seen,
You bring us joy.

You drift below the naked trees,
You softly dance in winter's breeze,
You flourish while all others freeze
And warm our hearts.
You mark the point when winter flees
And springtime starts.

Carol Coventry.

February Promises

February fill dyke, the proverb goes,
Torrents of rain and sometimes snow,
Yet this short month brings bright times, too,
With signs of spring as flowers grow.

Celandines with a glint of gold,
Willows and catkins adorning trees,
Delicate snowdrops carpet the ground
Daffodils nodding in the breeze.

Young lambs are gambolling down in the lea,
Every songbird is singing and building a nest,
The urge to raise young abounds everywhere
As God's earth stirs from her long, winter rest.

Saint Valentine's Day offers sweet new love
To the young tender heart of each girl and boy,
Though a sombre Ash Wednesday brings us to Lent
It will climax at Easter in renewal and joy.

George Hughes.

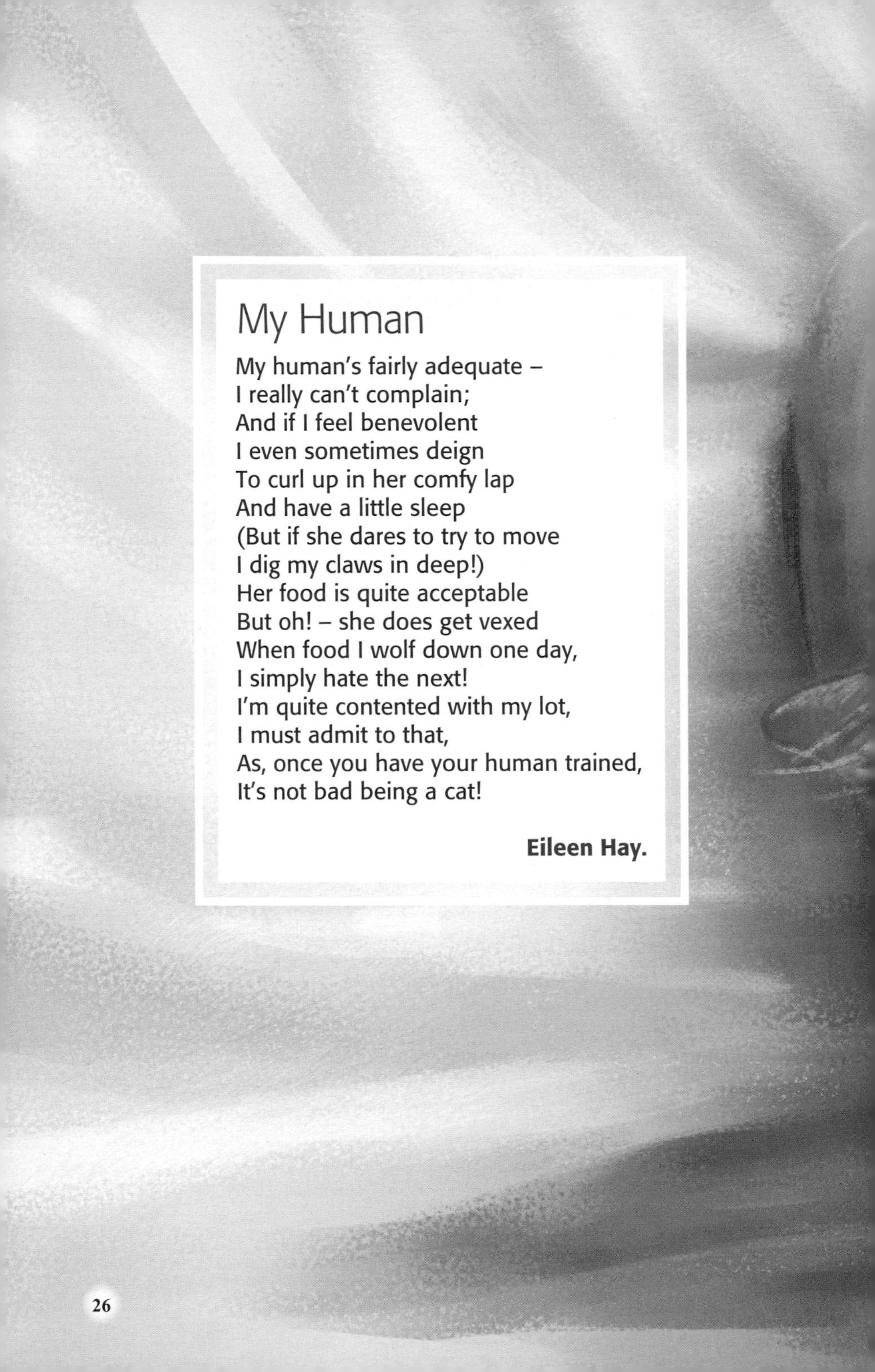

My Human

My human's fairly adequate –
I really can't complain;
And if I feel benevolent
I even sometimes deign
To curl up in her comfy lap
And have a little sleep
(But if she dares to try to move
I dig my claws in deep!)
Her food is quite acceptable
But oh! – she does get vexed
When food I wolf down one day,
I simply hate the next!
I'm quite contented with my lot,
I must admit to that,
As, once you have your human trained,
It's not bad being a cat!

Eileen Hay.

Springtime

At last the winter's chills retreat.
No icy winds to freeze our tears.
And numbness leaves our hands and feet,
While snowdrops show their dark green spears.

We wait, we watch and search the sky,
For sure enough through wind and rain
The swallows to our gardens fly,
Rebuilding their old nests again.

A tulip stirs then upward shoots.
A daffodil thrusts through the soil,
While germinating seeds make roots
And hibernating snakes uncoil.

But more importantly these days
We hope the olive-bearing dove
Will bring us peace through balmy haze
And fill our countryside with love.

James S. Stevenson.

My Favourite Weather

So what's my favourite weather? It's really hard to say;
Can anything be better than a gorgeous sunny day?

I do enjoy a windy day when leaves are whirling round,
Or rainy days when I can splash in puddles on the ground.

Fog is quite mysterious and hailstones are such fun,
While frosty days are crisp and clear, especially in the sun.

Though what about when snow has turned the world a dazzling white,
Or wild, dramatic thunderstorms – that glorious flash of light?

No; best is when the sun bursts through some dark clouds on the march,
And right across the sky there hangs a glorious rainbow arch.

Ewan Smith.

Dapper Little Sparrow

Dapper little sparrow
Perched upon a twig,
Ruffles up his feathers
Does a sort of jig.
Brightly looks about him,
Settles for a while
Gladdens up the morning
By giving me a smile.

Tricia Sturgeon.

Awakenings

Spring, when days lengthen and sun shines anew,
Wakening bluebells and crocuses, too.
Tulips and daffodils poised for display
To melt winter darkness, melt sadness away.
Pruning and digging, uprooting the weeds.
Preparing the ground for the gardeners' needs.
Sowing the crops and the seeds in the field,
To work towards harvest with bountiful yield.
Little white lambs to the hills will return.
Snow on the melt, to bolster the burn.
Rain on the days when the laundry needs dried.
Roots and new shoots that the sunshine supplied.
Snails and their trails and their shimmering route.
New life has begun – let ripen the fruit.

B.J. Fairweather.

Springing To Life

I REMEMBER, as a wee boy, I used to enjoy helping my dad in our garden at home in Glasgow. In fact, I actually persuaded him to let me have a little plot of my own to look after.

On reflection, I really don't think my efforts were very fruitful. I don't think very much blossomed forth from my wee patch! But at least I kept it tidy.

During the years of my ministry I had rather larger manse gardens to look after and, as time permitted, I did my best.

Following a particularly harsh winter, and in the first flush of spring, I was reminding the boys and girls in church one Sunday about all the frost and snow that had blanketed the earth not so very long ago, in the bleak midwinter, when earth was hard as iron.

At that time it would have been quite impossible to do much digging, but now that spring was in the air everyone could literally dig in and start to bring their gardens back to fruition.

"Isn't it remarkable, boys and girls," I said to them, "that the ground, the earth which has been the victim of all that winter frost and snow and ice, can nevertheless produce such lovely spring flowers such as daffodils and crocuses and tulips and snowdrops?"

In a way it is difficult to imagine how tiny bulbs could be growing away under the frozen, hard ground all through the winter. It's difficult to believe that lovely flowers would spring from such frozen, dead soil.

But then, this is one of the wonders of God's creation. As God looks after all of us above the ground, he looks after the tiny bulbs under the ground so that in his good time they shoot up, bringing with them new life and new colour.

Of course, new life is what Easter is all about, because it was at Eastertime that Jesus rose from the dead.

The people thought Jesus was dead after he had been crucified on the cross and put

iStock.

---

by Rev. Ian W.F. Hamilton.

▶ away in the sealed tomb. They never imagined for one minute that he would rise from the dead, just as we sometimes find it difficult to imagine the lovely flowers springing from dead soil.

But as the flowers in our gardens always spring to life, so, too, at Eastertime, does Jesus!

Many years ago someone managed to capture the whole meaning of Easter Day in a sentence.

"The grave was in a garden."

The person who wrote these words did so in the light of some words found in St John's gospel story, namely, "Now at the place where he had been crucified there was a garden, and in the garden, a new tomb."

The sentence "The grave was in a garden" seems to me to capture completely the mighty victory of God. The place of death opened into a place of life, because as we with hindsight look back on the grave and the garden, we see spring to light very clearly some of the things that made the friends of Jesus glad.

For instance, from the gospel garden, truth blossomed from treachery. Underlying all that Jesus had previously taught his disciples was his sureness of God Almighty, his unwavering certainty that in God's world truth was invincible.

Then suddenly God had let him down. Jesus relied on truth and it had seemingly failed him. His life had been snuffed out by political treachery and savage brutality.

That floored the friends of Jesus then, and it floors us now – until we experience the Easter message assuring us of the timelessness and unchangeableness of the One whose grave was in a garden, the One whose place of death became a place of life, the Living Truth, Jesus Christ.

And then, from the gospel garden there blossomed forth triumph over tragedy. Isn't it a rather amazing paradox that so great a tragedy as the cross turned out to be a victory?

Isn't it remarkable that such a denial of God became a revelation of God, that God could take this terrible thing and make it into the very instrument of his redemptive purposes?

Our world has many answers and many philosophies about the meaning of tragedy and heartbreak and sorrow, but no-one has ever answered the need in men and women as creatively and as triumphantly as Jesus Christ.

What we have in Christianity is not another explanation of pain and suffering, but rather a way of facing it, and a way of making it fruitful and of turning its tragedy into a ministry.

The victory of triumph over tragedy must surely gladden the hearts of

Christian disciples in every age.

The grave was in a garden, and life there was stronger than death!

There's someone in this universe mightily concerned about keeping life going, and he, at Eastertime, shows us again and again just how concerned he is. He lifts our spirits and gladdens our hearts beyond measure.

In the gospel garden, truth springs up over treachery, triumph springs up over tragedy, and not least, life eternal springs up over life temporal.

The grave was in a garden; the place of death opens, for us, today into a place of life . . . and tomorrow into a place of life everlasting.

Little did I think, as the wee boy tending his little plot in a suburban garden in Glasgow, that what I was about was of such deep, theological, everlasting and eternal significance.

The words of the poet written long-since sum it all up for us: "You are nearer God's heart in a garden than anywhere else on earth." ■

Nature's Calendar For Spring

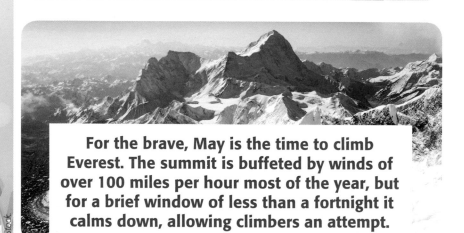

Spinach is ready to pick in late spring. In homage to famous spinach fan Popeye, the leaf-growing town of Crystal City in Texas erected a statue of him.

For the brave, May is the time to climb Everest. The summit is buffeted by winds of over 100 miles per hour most of the year, but for a brief window of less than a fortnight it calms down, allowing climbers an attempt.

iStock.

Baby elephants suck their trunks for comfort in the same way human children suck their thumbs.

Keep an eye for whether the oak or the ash comes into leaf first.
"If the oak before ash, we'll have a splash. Ash before oak, we're in for a soak," the old saying goes.

Tornado season in the United States reaches its peak in May. The highest wind speeds on earth were recorded in Oklahoma at 302 miles per hour.

Car Booting

Sunday morning, fine and fair,
Car booters all ready, seated in chairs,
Sun is out and sky is blue,
Buy or sell? It's up to you!

A torch, a bike and a jack-in-the-box,
Encyclopaedias, a big stuffed fox,
A stripy rug for the bedroom floor,
A handle for a kitchen door.

Kettles, toasters, an HD telly,
A bird's cage and a pair of wellies,
Dollies, toys, an old rocking horse,
Games and puzzles here, too, of course.

Old oak sideboard – could be antique!
Costume jewellery – let's take a peek.
A multi-coloured range of caps and hats,
A cute tea cosy in the shape of a cat.

Here, look – a lovely summer dress,
Pretty and floral, it's sure to impress.
A tasty aroma – eat all you can
From the hot dog stall and the burger van.

Trading outside in the warmth of the sun,
A car boot sale is such good fun.
We'll pack up now, it's half-past noon.
Same time next week: we'll see you soon!

S. Bee.

Cuckoo Time

Thoughts of May and hawthorn sweet
Remind me of the cuckoo,
Our feathered friend we soon shall greet,
Who'll hear him before I do?

We love to hear that sleepy tune
Despite our idle ways,
To country folk it means that soon
We'll have warm summer days!

So pray excuse their lack of care
To tend to their own young,
For spring is here; the time when
Nature welcomes everyone!

George Hughes.

Bluebells

Not really blue, but purple,
Mauve that fades into the blue;
Or blue that seems to melt and glow
Where sunlight filters through:
A river stretching far and wide –
A deep and azure sea –
Where words are drowned, made
  meaningless,
And thoughts at last run free.
A charm that weaves its magic spell
With sunlight through the trees;
Is any flower still growing wild
More beautiful than these?

Dawn Lawrence.

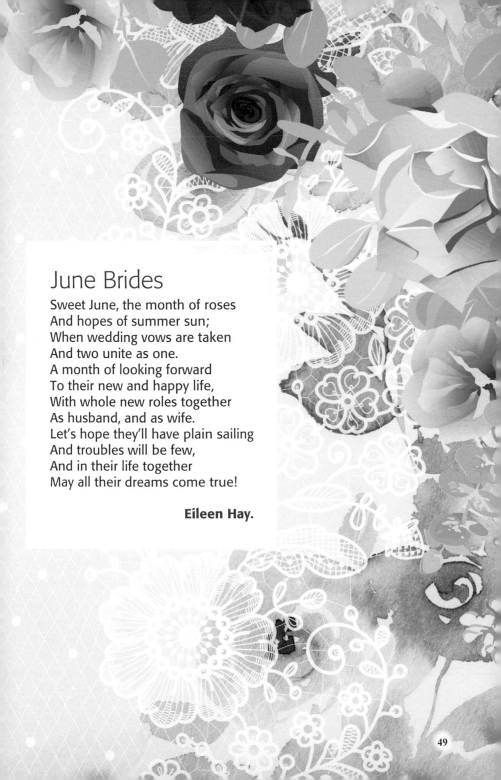

June Brides

Sweet June, the month of roses
And hopes of summer sun;
When wedding vows are taken
And two unite as one.
A month of looking forward
To their new and happy life,
With whole new roles together
As husband, and as wife.
Let's hope they'll have plain sailing
And troubles will be few,
And in their life together
May all their dreams come true!

Eileen Hay.

Under The Damson Tree

This seat around the damson tree:
It's slightly broken, I'll admit.
It's rustic, faded, needs some work;
Yet it's my favourite place to sit.

From here, I see the shrubs and trees
(I've let them grow a trifle tall),
The stones, the pond, the scattered logs,
The ivy clinging to the wall.

I stretch my legs out on the lawn:
It's getting long – could do with mowing –
But I don't mind meadow grass
Or buttercups and daisies growing.

Best of all, my visitors:
I watch the graceful birds arriving.
Shy hedgehogs and cheeky squirrels
And insects: busy, wild and thriving.

Maybe one day – in good time –
I'll clear it. Now I'll let it be.
I'll sit and watch, content and still,
Beneath my shady damson tree.

Emma Canning.

My Little Car

I've never owned a Bentley
Nor driven a Rolls-Royce,
My car is only tiny,
Yet it's my perfect choice.

I can't say it's the newest,
We've been friends for a while,
Sharing bumps along life's road
And joys with every smile.

It may look scratched and dented,
And, in places, slightly bruised,
But how it sings in freedom
As along the lanes we cruise!

Will we travel to the countryside
Or head off to the sea?
I wonder where we'll go today,
My little car and me.

Marion Cleworth.

53

A Picture-postcard Village

A picture-postcard village,
So picturesque and old,
Its cottages all crowned with thatch,
A pleasure to behold.

What sights and sounds those walls have known,
What tales of love and strife,
Of all the folk who lived within;
Their highs and lows of life.

In summertime the tourists come,
To walk the narrow lanes,
Buy souvenirs in quaint wee shops
With tiny window-panes.

They photograph the cottages,
Send postcards to their friends,
And patronise the tea-rooms,
From spring till summer's end.

But when the crowds have gone away,
And peace returns once more,
The village keeps its secrets still,
Just like in days of yore.

Rosemary Bennett.

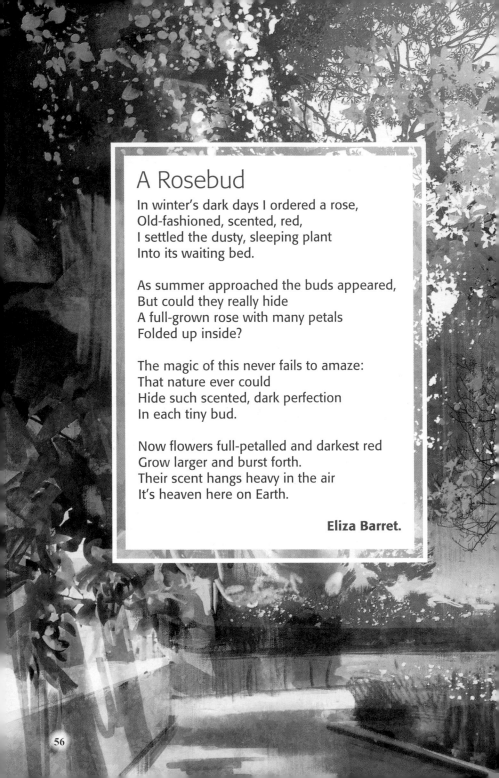

A Rosebud

In winter's dark days I ordered a rose,
Old-fashioned, scented, red,
I settled the dusty, sleeping plant
Into its waiting bed.

As summer approached the buds appeared,
But could they really hide
A full-grown rose with many petals
Folded up inside?

The magic of this never fails to amaze:
That nature ever could
Hide such scented, dark perfection
In each tiny bud.

Now flowers full-petalled and darkest red
Grow larger and burst forth.
Their scent hangs heavy in the air
It's heaven here on Earth.

Eliza Barret.

57

Change With The Seasons

WHAT'S your favourite time of year? I like to pride myself on being a reasonably decisive sort of person, but I must admit that this question always stumps me.

You see, my choice of answer will change with the seasons themselves.

Ask me that question in autumn, and I will undoubtedly answer, "Right now, of course!" What can be more satisfying than watching the fruit ripen ready for harvesting, and seeing the trees glowing in their gold and scarlet splendour?

What nicer way of spending a warm and sleepy afternoon than picking juicy blackberries, with the distant tang of leafy bonfire smoke hanging in the air?

At least, that would be my considered opinion until winter comes along. For despite a new chill to the days, there is often something rather magical about winter.

No longer hidden, we see the full beauty of the trees' graceful shapes, whilst any berries left on the twigs shine out like jewels.

There are winter walks we can take – perhaps along snowy country lanes, or down city roads, street lights gleaming on wet pavements, and shop windows filled with Christmas enchantments.

There is nothing like the wonder of a star-filled sky on a clear winter night, and once back indoors, there are warm fires to sit beside and, if we are lucky, hot chocolate to be drunk and sweet chestnuts to be roasted!

Which is why winter is undoubtedly my favourite season of the year – until, of course, spring begins. Spring can be the most modest of all seasons – at least to begin with. She creeps in so tentatively that we sometimes hardly realise her arrival.

Then we notice that there are new green buds on the branches, and new green shoots pushing upwards from the earth.

There is a new softness to the air, and before we know it, she is heralding her presence ▶

iStock.

By Maggie Ingall.

▶ with bright trumpets of daffodils and clamorous birdsong.

Yes, indeed, spring has absolutely to be the very best of all seasons!

But oh, dear, what's this? Right now I see the next season smiling at me from the wings, and my indecisiveness starts all over again!

I know that summer does indeed have an official start date, but for me it always feels that it's the festival of Pentecost which ushers in the real arrival of summer.

Coming seven weeks after Easter Sunday, Pentecost – or, as it is just as well known, Whitsunday – celebrates the time when the Holy Spirit descended upon Christ's Apostles, giving them the ability to speak other languages – the Gift of Tongues – which allowed them to start spreading the Christian message far and wide across the world.

Pentecost is a time of exultation and joy, which seems to be entirely appropriate to the arrival of summer.

With that in mind, perhaps it's not surprising that so many Whitsun traditions have grown up over the years. Even centuries ago, Whitsuntide, the week following Whitsunday, marked a brief lull in the agricultural cycle, giving a mediaeval villein or peasant farmer a rare few days of rest from their labours.

In the not-so-distant-past, factory and mill workers would also be given a much-needed week's holiday away from their workplaces.

Celebrations such as Whitfairs have been – and still are – held throughout not just Britain, but in many parts of the world.

In Poland, the houses are frequently decorated with freshly cut green branches. In Hungary, games are held to test skills in archery and horsemanship.

In Germany many public areas are adorned with red flowers as a vivid reminder of the fire of the Holy Spirit. And in this country we have fêtes and picnics, Morris dancing, cheese-rolling and other special sporting events.

There are Whit Walks, where church and chapel congregations gather together to parade through the streets, often carrying beautifully woven banners and accompanied by local choirs and brass bands. And, of course, Whit Week has traditionally been the most popular time for weddings and baptisms – and new clothes!

My good friend Beryl fondly remembers how, as a child, this time of year always marked the purchase (or the making) of a new summer outfit, complete with white socks and smart brown crepe-soled sandals.

"The best part," she told me, "was that I would then be taken to have my new finery admired by my grandparents and aunts – who, if I was very lucky, would reward me with a shilling to spend!"

Although Pentecost may herald the start of summer, happily it is just the start, for there is so much more to come.

Just as the rosebuds slowly unfurl into beautiful blooms, so the days slowly unfurl into glorious weeks. Even rain showers can't be too unwelcome when we know that they're the source of life and health to a wealth of colourful plants and shrubs.

And when the sun does shine, it truly is good to get outside and enjoy the season, whether on a beach or in the countryside, in a park or in your own garden.

There is only one rule that I make for myself, and that is not to feel guilty about seizing every moment that I possibly can simply to sit back and enjoy it.

As the philanthropist and scientist John Lubbock is quoted as saying, "Rest is not idleness, and to lie sometimes on the grass under trees on a summer's day, listening to the murmur of the water, or watching the clouds float across the sky, is by no means a waste of time."

I entirely agree – and I do very much hope that you, too, will get the chance to lie on the grass and enjoy the summer! ∎

Nature's Calendar For *Summer*

June takes its name from Juno, the Roman goddess of marriage, which makes it good luck to be wed in this month.

Peas are tasty and ready to eat right now. A cup of peas also contains as much protein as an entire egg.

Adult birds will be out now gathering goodies for their young. Many varieties of bird eat seeds and berries and have to supplement the diet of their young with insects, to provide enough protein for their growth.

Yosemite National Park in California is worth visiting before the schools go off in mid-July. In the park there are 500 giant sequoias which are the largest living things on the planet.

Comedian Billy Connolly once said, "There are two seasons in Scotland: June and winter."

Little Old Churches

I love little old churches
With stories to tell;
With coloured glass windows,
A tower and a bell.

Those hidden away
For long years where they stood
Often lonely, forgotten,
In lanes or a wood.

Those with old barrelled ceilings,
A small font and door,
That have just enough room
For about twenty-four;

Where bats roost in the rafters,
And only birds sing;
Where a deep sense of peace
Pervades everything.

There are churches I know
Both majestic and tall,
But these smallest churches
I love most of all.

They were much more important
To those few who came,
Who walked there for miles
Through woodland and lane.

And each little church
Has surely been blessed
By those simple souls
Who once loved them best.

Dawn Lawrence.

Summer In The Garden

I'm sitting in my garden, it's looking at its best,
I've had a busy morning, I'm glad to be at rest.
I've got some chocolate biscuits, I've made a mug of tea,
It's lovely doing nothing . . . but hey, what's that I see?
A weed that shouldn't be there – oh, dear, that has to go,
Then back to claim my deckchair – ah, this is nice – but, oh!
I've just observed those roses – dead-heading overdue!
And now I come to notice, the grass needs cutting, too.
So this is my dilemma; it's tricky, I confess,
To laze, or start to labour? I think I'll let you guess!

Maggie Ingall.

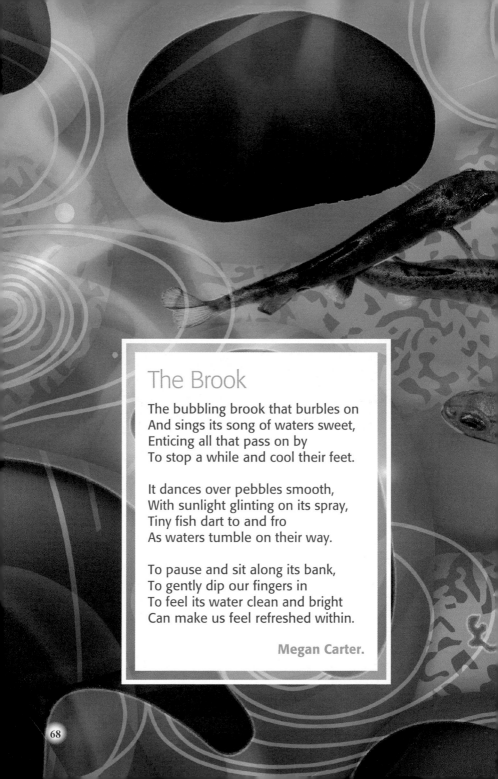

The Brook

The bubbling brook that burbles on
And sings its song of waters sweet,
Enticing all that pass on by
To stop a while and cool their feet.

It dances over pebbles smooth,
With sunlight glinting on its spray,
Tiny fish dart to and fro
As waters tumble on their way.

To pause and sit along its bank,
To gently dip our fingers in
To feel its water clean and bright
Can make us feel refreshed within.

Megan Carter.

Unexpected Love

The summer rain fell softly to the earth,
And ran in rivulets across the dry terrain.
The land received a promise of rebirth
And tears cascaded down the window-pane.

The shower subsided, all was quiet and still
Then, as a gift, a perfume filled the air.
A sweet, sharp smell, all its own, until
It drowned my senses like a thankful prayer.

Petrichor, the word from ancient Greek;
Fluid in the veins of those Greek gods.
Nature's fragrance, released with a mystique,
A blessing after rain; like love against the odds.

Meg Stokes.

71

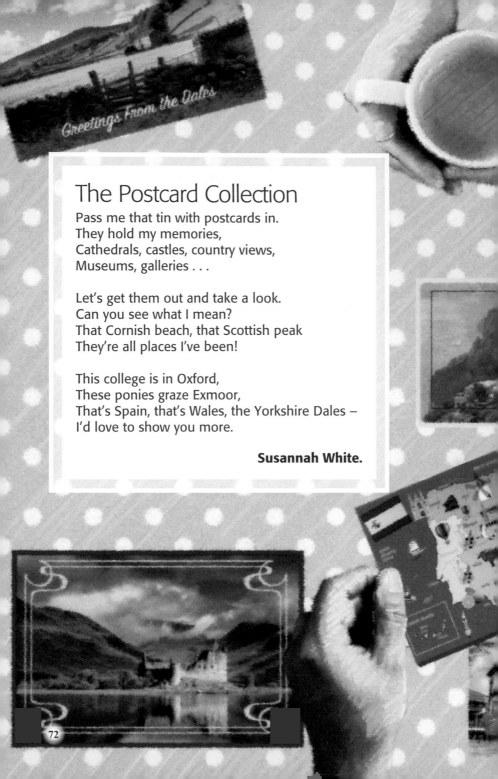

The Postcard Collection

Pass me that tin with postcards in.
They hold my memories,
Cathedrals, castles, country views,
Museums, galleries . . .

Let's get them out and take a look.
Can you see what I mean?
That Cornish beach, that Scottish peak
They're all places I've been!

This college is in Oxford,
These ponies graze Exmoor,
That's Spain, that's Wales, the Yorkshire Dales –
I'd love to show you more.

Susannah White.

Greetings From the Dales

A Garden Of Memories

I take my seat in the summer sun,
Ignoring the chores that could be done.
The fountain glistens as it flows
And all around the garden grows.

I'm lost in thought as time goes by,
Flowers grow and flowers die
And loved ones, too, have passed away
But memories linger, every day.

Every plant and every bloom
Lift my spirits from any gloom.
The honeysuckle from Jenny's plot,
Susan gave me the forget-me-not.

Ann shared fragrant lemon thyme
And the apple tree that's in its prime.
Cuttings from others who have passed away,
And though the plants may soon decay

They will return as good as new,
And one day I'll greet my loved ones, too,
And we'll embrace in the summer sun,
In my garden of memories, when the chores are done.

Anne Hooker.

Time For Tea

In a tearoom, a table's set.
Water boiled, not ready yet.
Rose-pink tiny china cups,
Ladies sip slow, no big gulps.

Shall we choose? It looks divine!
Scones and jam, a favourite of mine,
Chocolate eclairs piped with cream,
Sweet lover's delight, an afternoon
   dream.

Soft sandwiches of delicate cucumber,
This taste of England I'll always
   remember.
What remains for ever in my heart –
A classic, perfect strawberry tart.

Muffins and crumpets, Battenburg cake
Must have taken hours to bake!
I hesitate, look hard and linger –
Butterfly bun or a sugar iced finger?

S. Bee.

Love Is In The Air

SUMMERTIME in North Donegal is just beautiful. Our rugged coastline and beaches are second to none. The hotels are full, the caravan parks and coffee shops are buzzing. And for some, romance is in the air!

Summertime is wedding season, and every year I have a few in the diary. Most couples like to come to the meeting house for their ceremony, but occasionally we get asked to do services elsewhere.

I remember one on a suitably laid out open-air hotel terrace overlooking the ocean just above Marble Hill beach.

It was a scorcher of a day and, between the idyllic setting and the fact that many of the gentlemen present were Scottish and dressed in kilts, it turned out rather spectacular. We even had a piper!

At weddings I usually have three Scripture readings.

The first is from the Old Testament Song of Songs, a passionate love poem set at a younger King Solomon's wedding to his beautiful peasant bride.

It's a classic romance involving the King disguising himself as a shepherd to woo a girl from more modest circumstances.

They fall deeply in love, and before long comes the day when he returns in majesty to bring her to the royal palace for the wedding.

Of course, for love to last and deepen we need more than passion, so I also read, from the Apostle Paul's 1 Corinthians 13, that famous passage describing love. Loving relationships need mutual commitment and faithful, ongoing nourishing!

I often finish with a reading such as 1 John 4 v 7-12, which specifically speaks of God and his Son as the strong, deep, self-sacrificing source of all love. Every aspect of life benefits from a positive relationship with him!

Old Testament prophets spoke of God being like a husband to the nation of Israel. The New Testament builds on this idea of God's people being betrothed or married to our Lord. ▶

iStock.

By Rev. Andrew Watson.

Jesus is described as a bridegroom; therefore, his Church is his "beloved", the bride in whom he delights.

New Testament Jewish weddings were different from how we do things nowadays. Here, usually, the groom and his family and guests arrive first and wait, and the last to arrive is the bride.

In first-century Palestine it was the other way around. The bride prepared herself and waited at home until the groom came to bring her to his parents' house to begin the ceremony and celebrations.

This makes sense of Jesus's parable of the wise and foolish bridesmaids who are waiting for the arrival of the groom so that things can get underway.

Jesus is teaching his Church to live in readiness for his coming in glory to judge the living and the dead and gather his precious people to his Father's heavenly home.

This will be the climax of the ages, the end of human history as we've known it. People need to be prepared.

At a fundamental level Jesus's parable is an alarm bell of warning – get ready, for the day is coming. If we're doing something wrong we need to stop.

If there's something good we should be doing, let's begin!

If we need to make peace with God or our neighbour, let's do it now!

That being said, this picture from Scripture gives people of faith a very beautiful picture of encouragement and assurance.

How's our self-esteem? Do we feel worthy of sacrifice? Do we know anyone who would give their life for us?

Hold on! Someone already has!

"Husbands, love your wives just as Christ loved the church and gave himself up for her, to make her holy," the Apostle Paul writes.

At Calvary it was as if Jesus said, "I don't want eternity without my beloved. I lay down my life that she might be saved and purified and made fit for my Father's house for ever!"

Despite our many faults, the Church is beloved, treasured by our Lord!

There is healing in this. We may be undervalued, even abused by others. Our own sin and failure may plague our conscience and tempt us toward self-doubt and loathing, but the Son of God calls us his beloved and suffered that we might be forgiven and welcomed in God's family.

Such generous love is rejuvenating, intoxicating. It makes us want to sing! It makes us want to live! The Christian religion has always had this element of rejoicing and thanksgiving as we bask each day in the redeeming love of Jesus.

It helps us live our lives with a sense of anticipation. Everyone has some trouble and heartache in the short-term – Jesus told us to expect

that – but we are people who are looking forward eagerly to a wedding. Ours!

The bride is waiting, longing for the time when her husband will come for her and the two will become one. Love will be shared, consummated, celebrated and enjoyed as long as they both shall live.

Christians are looking forward eagerly to welcoming our returning Lord, to meeting our Saviour face to face, and resting in the shelter of his love for ever with no spoiling barrier of sin.

A bride has eyes only for her husband. She has no interest in others. She will naturally want to make herself as attractive as possible, pleasing for him.

Likewise the Church. As we await our Lord the heavenly bridegroom, we must seek to be beautiful in his eyes with words, actions and attitudes that conform to all that he loves and reveals in his word.

The Church is the bride of the Lord Jesus. We are his beloved for whom he laid down his life. We are living in anticipation of his coming to bring us home and our being with him for ever. ∎

iStock.

Nature's Calendar For *Summer*

Plums are grown on every continent except Antarctica, and are one of our oldest cultivated foods. Their stones have been found on archaeological sites with the remains of olives, grapes and figs.

Originally the sixth month of the Roman calendar, August was renamed in 8 BC after Augustus Caesar.

iStock.

When the French Riviera heaves with the heat and summer tourists, the Alpine lakes of France are quieter and just as lovely. Annecy, on the lake of the same name, is known for its cobbled streets and pastel houses.

As places like Alaska rapidly move into their autumn, it's not uncommon for the first snows to dust the mountains in August.

Henry James, author of "The Portrait Of A Lady", once said, "Summer afternoon – summer afternoon; to me those have always been the two most beautiful words in the English language."

Dialects

I love the Dorset dialect, that warm and honeyed tongue,
So different from those dulcet tones – the way Welsh words
  are sung.

But go down to the West Country, where the cider apples
  grow;
One can't mistake that dialect, it's one I'll always know.

The Irish have their lilting speech, the Scots can melt my heart;
But the Dorset dialect, I find, will always stand apart.

In Somerset the same is true, they have this lazy drawl
And roll their "r"s disarmingly, which I love best of all.

My window cleaner has this gift of captivating me,
He simply smiles, he doffs his cap, and says, "And how be ye?"

Dawn Lawrence.

The Village Dance

It's such a popular event
Folk come from far and near,
From east and west, all dressed their best,
And brimming with good cheer!

While groups of women stand and chat,
Young girls stand shy and coy,
And couples dance to a band that was grand
When Adam was a boy!

The ladies of a certain age
Conduct themselves with pride,
With stately gait and backs so straight
Stout chest to chest they glide!

The walls all shake and faces glow
As freely flows the beer,
We all unite to vote this night
The highlight of the year!

Eileen Hay.

The Last Roses

Too soon we know we're near the end
Of lazy, languid summer days;
Already nights are drawing in
And sunrise brings a misty haze.

The roses now are past their best
And fallen petals on the ground
Create a perfumed bridal show –
A velvet carpet all around.

It's sad to see them fade and die,
To know that autumn's almost here,
But they'll be back, these works of art
With glorious blooms again next year.

Eileen Hay.

The Orchard

Late sunlight in the orchard
Has tipped the trees with gold,
A moment of perfection
Before the year grows old.

The fruit has long since ripened,
The apples, pears and plums
Are safely stored and bottled
Before the winter comes.

And so, for now, the orchard
Rests, drowsing and at peace,
A few stray leaves drift downwards,
The last of summer's lease.

Such days – so short, so fleeting –
Will soon be left behind,
But just for now, this moment,
The hour is soft and kind.

Maggie Ingall.

Food Galore

I'm paying tribute to British fare,
Cooked and baked with passion and flair.
Lots and lots of delightful dishes,
All completely divine and delicious.

Food galore, come take your pick:
Thick rice pudding and spotted dick;
Cottage pie and beans on toast,
Yorkshire pudding, Sunday roast.

Bubble and squeak, corned beef hash,
Liver and onions, bangers and mash,
Home-made honey, thickly spread,
A slice of chunky doorstep bread.

Fish and chips with mushy peas,
Crackers and cheddar, more cheese,
  please!
Stew and dumplings, mustard and ham,
Sticky sponge pudding, oozing with jam.

I hope that you will all agree
British food's a treat, you see,
A comfort eat, and tasty, too,
A good hot meal for me and you!

S. Bee.

The Butterfly Brooch

I find a little box, long lost,
And slide aside the golden clasp.
What does it hide? What waits inside?
What secrets lie within my grasp?

I lift its tiny leather lid
To see a velvet nest of red
And pinned inside, a silver brooch,
A butterfly with wings outspread.

His green glass eyes hold specks of dust.
I fetch a cloth to clear each mote,
Until his painted rainbow wings,
Shine bright for flight, pinned on my coat.

Susannah White.

Simple Signs

There is a nip in the air today,
As the breezes make the branches sway,
The leaves have lost their sylvan sheen,
And the lawn does not look quite so green.

The flowers are not standing straight,
And the roses wilt at the garden gate,
Swifts and swallows, martins, too,
Have flown in search of climates new,

The cuckoo's call is heard no more,
And larks to heaven no longer soar,
All the simple signs to say,
Autumn now is on its way . . .

Brian H. Gent.

Fox In The Mist

I'd reached the summit of the hill, the sun now red and low,
Grey shawls of misty gauze now draped the valley spread
  below.
Before too long the thickening mist came creeping up the hill
Until I felt it in my throat, engulfing, damp and chill.

An ancient wood adjoined the path, and as I walked with care
A silent fox slipped from the trees, and paused, and sniffed
  the air.
I froze and stood there, statue still; he slowly turned his head;
His eyes were gleaming in the mist, his coat a greyish red.

Quite unafraid, he held my gaze and then, with some disdain,
He turned, and vanished in the trees, and was not seen again.

Eileen Hay.

from the Manse Window

The Gifts Of God

THIS morning I was reading in my bible about Hannah, the mother of the prophet Samuel.

You may remember that she was barren and her husband's other wife, who was able to have children, taunted her.

So Hannah prayed fervently for a child and promised God that if she had a son he would be dedicated to his service.

She did fall pregnant and had Samuel.

After he was weaned Hannah took him up to the house of the Lord at Shiloh and left him there with these words: "So now I give him to the Lord. For the whole of his life he shall be given over to the Lord."

What follows is Hannah's wonderful prayer full of praise to God.

If you read it you can almost see the tears of joy in her eyes as the words spill out of her mouth.

It's almost impossible to understand how a woman could give up a longed-for child and do it with such joy.

But that is what obedience and faithfulness brings – an incredible joy.

To give sacrificially with an open heart and a desire to please God brings a joy nothing in the world can compare to.

To be doing the will of God is a wonderful thing.

Many years ago, when I was a student in London, I ran out of money 10 days before the end of term.

I prayed about it.

A friend was walking along the street and suddenly on the pavement saw a £10 note (a lot of money in those days!) and knew that it was for me.

That money got me through the last few days and, the day before I was due to return home for the holiday, I went to church and tipped every last coin left over back into the collection plate in thanks for God's provision.

It filled me with tremendous joy to do that as I acknowledged God's faithfulness.

By Rev. Susan Sarapuk.

iStock.

▶ Now, of course, that doesn't compare to Hannah's experience of giving up her child.

But the principle is the same – God provides, and out of that we give in a freewill offering and it results in joy.

Jesus talked about how his joy would be in his disciples. It was a different kind of joy from that of the world.

It wasn't about getting things or being successful; it was about being a servant, of letting go of things, of being content with what you have and knowing your place in the kingdom.

It was about being filled with the desire to hear only one accolade: "Well done, good and faithful servant."

There were tough lessons the disciples had to learn before they proved the truth of Jesus's words and the same is true for us.

We can't do the big things until we've learned to trust God in the small things.

Hannah must have been trusting God for a long time so that, when the big thing came along, she was able to give sacrificially in a freewill offering.

She did it with joy and rejoiced over it.

Hannah went on to have more children.

That's the wonderful thing about giving to God — he always gives back when we are generous.

"Give and it will be given to you. A good measure, pressed down, shaken together and running over will be poured into your lap," Jesus said.

Samuel became one of Israel's greatest prophets. Hannah's obedience fulfilled the purposes of God.

We are reminded that everything fits into God's plan if we are obedient, and obedience brings a joy to which nothing else can compare. ■

Nature's Calendar For *Autumn*

Artichokes are actually flowers that are yet to bloom, and are part of the sunflower family. They have one of the highest levels of antioxidants in any vegetable.

For the birds that don't migrate, early autumn is a calmer time. Our resident birds give up squabbling over territory and prefer to settle in for the evening after sunset.

The month of September, so named because it was the seventh month of the old Roman calendar, has more babies born in it than any other time of year.

Every year, the Newquay Fish Festival celebrates the Cornish town's long heritage of fishing and seafood in September. The town got its name when a new quay was built in the 15th century to form the harbour.

There are two types of brent geese – one with a dark belly and one with a light. The darker ones fly to southern England in mid-September, and spend the summer in Siberia. The light ones go to Ireland, and then head off to Canada for the summer.

Happiness

The fire is blazing brightly,
The cat is on my knee,
And I'm curled up on the sofa
With a cup of hot, sweet tea.
I'm halfway through a good book,
A stew bubbles away,
The peace and quiet's lovely;
Just another perfect day.

Susan Bennett.

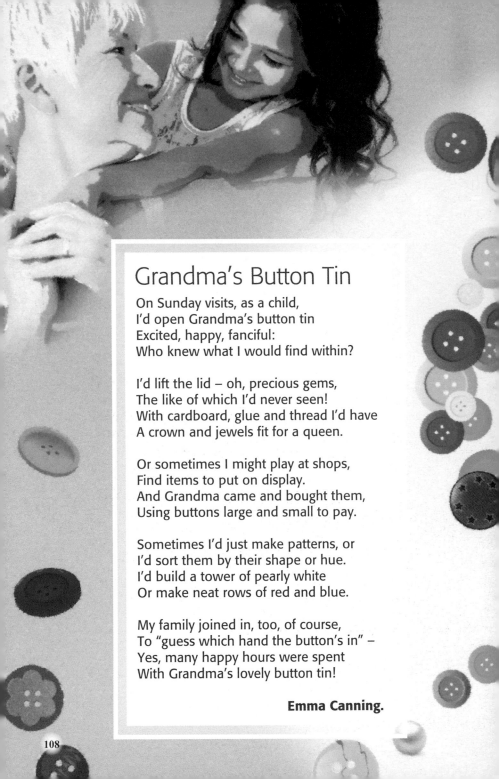

Grandma's Button Tin

On Sunday visits, as a child,
I'd open Grandma's button tin
Excited, happy, fanciful:
Who knew what I would find within?

I'd lift the lid – oh, precious gems,
The like of which I'd never seen!
With cardboard, glue and thread I'd have
A crown and jewels fit for a queen.

Or sometimes I might play at shops,
Find items to put on display.
And Grandma came and bought them,
Using buttons large and small to pay.

Sometimes I'd just make patterns, or
I'd sort them by their shape or hue.
I'd build a tower of pearly white
Or make neat rows of red and blue.

My family joined in, too, of course,
To "guess which hand the button's in" –
Yes, many happy hours were spent
With Grandma's lovely button tin!

Emma Canning.

October

First frost and crispy leaves are things
At autumn time October brings;
Rowan jelly, apples, too,
Plums that tingle teeth right through;

Picking sloes to make good wine,
Damson jam that tastes divine;
Pumpkins, too, bring obvious praise
To brighten darker autumn days;

And then it's just that time of year
When woollen scarves and gloves appear;
When duvets pop out from the gloom
Of cupboards, drawers or attic room;

And Hallowe'en for everyone
Just makes October lots of fun.

Dawn Lawrence.

The Knitted Doll

It was the annual Homecraft Fair
With hand-made goods on every stall;
On one, in bobble hat and plaits,
Sat just the quaintest knitted doll!

Because she had the sweetest face
I took my money out to pay,
Then thought a child should have first chance
So thought it best to walk away.

I guess that most small girls today
Like dolls with curls that they can style,
And satin dresses they can swap,
And fluttering eyes and painted smile.

Because, as closing time approached
And I longed for a cup of tea,
She was still there, the knitted doll,
As if she waited just for me!

So now she has her own small chair
And sits, hands folded on her knee,
Her red-wool smile just cheers my day –
I'm sure she's where she's meant to be!

Eileen Hay.

Autumn Serenade

The autumn leaves are glorious
With russet, red and gold,
A legacy from summertime,
Such beauty to behold.

The distant hills have purple hues,
Soft mist lies on the moor,
The smell of wood smoke on the air
All help our spirits soar.

A gentle breeze comes creeping in
Recalling summer days,
And in the wood the small birds sing
Their autumn songs of praise.

And though the days grow shorter now
Let winter be delayed,
As we rejoice in sights and sounds
Of autumn's serenade.

Iris Hesselden.

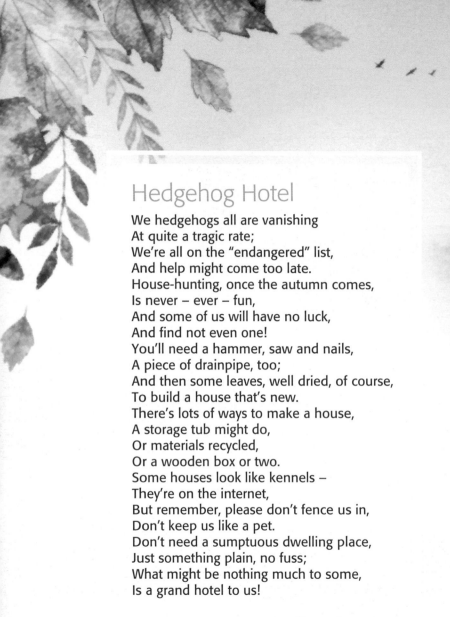

Hedgehog Hotel

We hedgehogs all are vanishing
At quite a tragic rate;
We're all on the "endangered" list,
And help might come too late.
House-hunting, once the autumn comes,
Is never – ever – fun,
And some of us will have no luck,
And find not even one!
You'll need a hammer, saw and nails,
A piece of drainpipe, too;
And then some leaves, well dried, of course,
To build a house that's new.
There's lots of ways to make a house,
A storage tub might do,
Or materials recycled,
Or a wooden box or two.
Some houses look like kennels –
They're on the internet,
But remember, please don't fence us in,
Don't keep us like a pet.
Don't need a sumptuous dwelling place,
Just something plain, no fuss;
What might be nothing much to some,
Is a grand hotel to us!

Dawn Lawrence.

Golden Days

The hazy green of summer
Has turned to autumn gold.
In this season's blazing splendour
We see new charms unfold.

Tinge of fire festoons the trees,
Crisp leaves come fluttering down,
We're kicking up the piles
Of ochre, red and brown.

The thrill of spiky conker fruit
Lying hidden in the earth,
The eager youngsters searching long
To get their treasure's worth.

There's magic in the twilight,
The burnish, before the snow
Mellow moments for sweet reflection
As we bask in firelight's glow.

Dorothy McGregor.

Refresh And Renew

AUTUMN is a season of huge contrasts. On the one hand, we have the "season of mists and mellow fruitfulness" so eloquently described by the poet John Keats, together with the glorious show of autumn colours our trees have put on in recent years.

On the other hand, we experience the fading of the year in the encroaching darkness, as the days grow ever shorter.

Both of these faces of autumn seem light years away at this moment, as I'm writing this piece in the middle of one of the longest heatwaves in living memory.

Yet despite the heat, the year has turned and the nights are beginning once again to draw in, even though we hardly notice it.

It wasn't always the case. Before the widespread arrival of electric light in the early 20th century, our forebears knew nothing but the regular rhythms of night and day, summer and winter.

Work in the fields would begin as the sun rose and cease when it set;

and the hours of darkness were for sleep. I have no wish to glamorise bygone times, as life for those who worked the land or in factories was unquestionably harsh.

But there was, nevertheless, a natural rhythm to life that was unquestioned, and with which people knew themselves to be in tune.

With the advent of electric light and the rapid technological advances of the last century, all that has changed. Now we can have light twenty-four hours a day, and internet technology means we can be in touch with anyone, anywhere in the world, instantly.

Some years ago there was even a horrific suggestion that we should put a gigantic mirror in space, to reflect the sun's rays back to us twenty-four hours a day!

Thankfully no-one seems to have taken that idea any further, but it offers us an indication of just how much we have become detached from the daily and seasonal rhythms that were natural to ▶

iStock.

By Rev. Barbara Mosse.

▶ our ancestors.

Consequently, we do not accept or easily understand any signs of these primitive rhythms in our own bodies: we expect, and are expected, to move in step with the ever-increasing speed of things, and we worry if our bodies seem unable to keep up with the frenetic pace of life.

The Bible has some wisdom to offer us on this matter.

"For everything there is a season," the writer of the Old Testament book Ecclesiastes says, "and a time for every matter under heaven: a time to be born, and a time to die; a time to plant, and a time to pluck up what is planted."

The passage goes on to cover, among other life experiences, the times for breaking down and building up, for war and peace, for speaking and for keeping silence.

The writer has a vision of the natural rhythm that runs through all of the times of our lives, and the wisdom and inner peace which comes when we are able to recognise and accept that rhythm.

It is natural for our bodies to indicate a need to slow down and ease the pace of life as we move towards the later months of the year, or the later years of our lives.

The pattern remains present in nature, for those who have eyes to see. The visible glory of our plants dies away, and the work of growth and renewal retreats underground.

Many animals enter a period of hibernation, which allows their bodies to rest, and to protect and renew their inner resources so that they will be ready for the fresh challenges of the coming spring.

Although we do not hibernate, our bodies, if we allow them, will naturally slow down as we move towards the autumn and winter months, conflicting strongly with society's pressure to remain as busy as possible.

I don't know whether it's anything to do with having been a November baby, but I always find my heart lifting as the days begin to shorten, in opposition to almost everyone amongst whom I have lived and worked.

We like to believe we are creatures of the light – and, in many ways, we are – but we also need the down-time of the dark so that our bodies may recoup their energies and maintain a healthy and balanced rhythm.

We may have succeeded in subduing the primitive rhythms inherited from our ancestors, but they still lie deep within us. They continue to play a different tune from the one our technological advances and worship of the god of progress seem to dictate.

So, as we approach the darkest time of the year, perhaps we can learn from Jesus's teaching on the seed growing unseen in the earth.

When it seems that all is dead and nothing around us is happening, the seed, hidden in the earth, is secretly growing and renewing itself.

We, too, are offered that opportunity to allow God, in the silence and privacy of our down-time, to refresh and renew us in his pattern and likeness. ■

Nature's Calendar For *Autumn*

Pomegranates come into season through autumn. The name "pomegranate" means "seeded apple".

The dying back of plant leaves in late autumn mean that you can see the highways and byways used by animals through woodland and the countryside. Long white and black hairs on these paths might indicate badgers in the area.

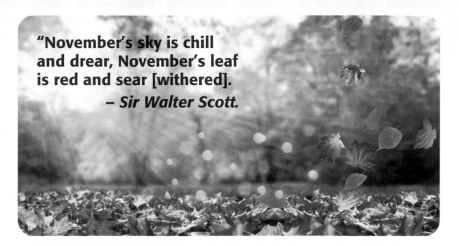

"November's sky is chill and drear, November's leaf is red and sear [withered].
– Sir Walter Scott.

According to the Greeks, Persephone was abducted by Hades in autumn. Her mother, Demeter, was the goddess of the harvest. As a result of her grief, all the crops die in the autumn only to return – when Persephone was returned – in the spring.

If you have nesting boxes for birds in the garden, now's a good time of year to clear them out. The birds have gone, so get them clean for spring and reduce the chances of any parasites spending the winter inside.

Sunset

The sky was glowing, radiant,
The colours luminescent,
Such swathes of orange, lilac, flame,
Just dazzlingly fluorescent.

Against this backdrop, rising high,
The turreted church tower
Stood out so tall and black and strong
In that bright sunset hour.

And in the distance, silently,
A "V" of geese was winging,
And as I watched this timeless scene
The church bells started ringing.

Eileen Hay.

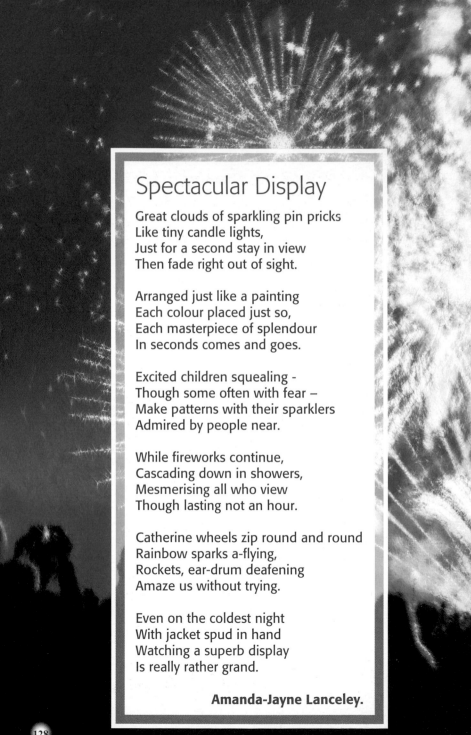

Spectacular Display

Great clouds of sparkling pin pricks
Like tiny candle lights,
Just for a second stay in view
Then fade right out of sight.

Arranged just like a painting
Each colour placed just so,
Each masterpiece of splendour
In seconds comes and goes.

Excited children squealing -
Though some often with fear –
Make patterns with their sparklers
Admired by people near.

While fireworks continue,
Cascading down in showers,
Mesmerising all who view
Though lasting not an hour.

Catherine wheels zip round and round
Rainbow sparks a-flying,
Rockets, ear-drum deafening
Amaze us without trying.

Even on the coldest night
With jacket spud in hand
Watching a superb display
Is really rather grand.

Amanda-Jayne Lanceley.

Remembering

The biggest congregation
With which the church was ever blessed,
Some wore smart, pressed uniforms,
Some wore their Sunday best;
Some solemnly bore standards,
Some wore medals on their chest;

Some wore faded berets,
Some bedecked in golden braid,
Some stood straight and tall,
Some only stood with aid.
All sombre, all reflecting,
All heads bowing as they prayed.

Eleven o'clock, a silence fell,
Silence so profound,
That, as poppy petals dropped
Each was heard to hit the ground.
Silence observed completely,
Until the bugle sound.

Then came the hymns and anthems,
Then chapters and verses read,
A sermon was delivered
And heartfelt prayers were said.
While blood-red poppy petals lay
As lay the fallen dead.

Carol Coventry.

The Storm

Yesterday the calm and today the storm.
The sea is angry and the boats are tossed.
Gulls ride the waves, they are unafraid
To be seen, and the next moment – lost.

Wintry shafts stream through the clouds;
The bright azure waves have not a trace
Of mercy, and their foaming mouths throw up
A froth, as white and delicate as lace.

They beat the shore with wrathful joy,
The storm does not allow them sleep
Till finally they fall, tired out,
To the unknown caverns of the deep.

Kate Blackadder.

Winter Of Discontent

Fog and snow and endless rain,
Wintertime is here again,
And so, you ask, will I complain?
Well, yes, I think I might!

The sun is weak, the wind is strong,
The days are short, the nights are long,
The gloomy hours just drag along,
And give us no delight.

Perhaps it's time to change my view,
And think of things I like to do,
For winter must hold pleasures, too,
To make the months more bright.

Frozen lanes with icy spark,
Graceful branches, bare and stark,
Early dusk and home by dark.
As all the world turns white.

Glowing fires and toast for tea,
Books to read and friends to see,
So perhaps I might agree
That winter is all right!

Maggie Ingall.

135

Rosy Robin's Visit

Good morning, little robin,
Sitting on my wall,
Did you come to cheer me?
How nice of you to call.

You're quite a lovely fellow
With your brilliantly red breast,
Are you looking for some twigs
To help you build your nest?

Where is Mrs Robin
On this bright sunny morn?
Is she eating all the crumbs
That are scattered on the lawn?

I love to hear you singing
High up in your tree.
A delightful song of happiness
And such a joy to see.

Avril Hooper.

Winter Hyacinths

The heady scent of hyacinths
Brings thoughts of long ago,
And childhood Scottish winters
When the ground was deep in snow.

I'd watch my mother plant the bowls
Then tend each lovely bloom
So that on snowy winter days
Their perfume filled each room.

I plant them now with thoughts of her
And know that they will bring
On dull and dismal winter days
The thought of coming spring.

Eileen Hay.

The Christmas Market

The market square is quite transformed
With strings of coloured baubles
And light from Christmas lanterns
Is reflected in the cobbles.

The air smells like a forest glade
With Christmas trees and holly,
And buskers play some lively tunes,
Their music bright and jolly!

Some stalls sell turkeys, hams and beef
To please discerning foodies,
At others, mince-pies, puddings, cakes –
All kinds of festive goodies!

The local hostelry sells beer
From huge iron-banded barrels,
And young and happy revellers
Sing merry off-key carols!

It's such a happy place to be,
Just filled with joy and laughter
And hopefully that spirit stays
For Christmas, and long after.

Eileen Hay.

Getting Comfortable

ARE you sitting comfortably? I'm not. As I type I am sitting in an ornate, high-backed, wooden chair with padded arm rests that I rescued from a church renovation several years ago. I gave the pastor a donation to the church's overseas ministry and took the chair home.

Actually, what I felt I was taking home were the sermons that had been composed in it over the decades, the problems that had been wrestled with and resolved in it, the prayers that had gone heavenward from it.

I love this old chair, and it has served me well, but if it ever was comfortable, it isn't now. And, strangely, that works. If it was more comfortable I might sit in it longer, wasting time instead of working.

Our comforts are often also distractions. Which might go some little way towards explaining why people and societies going through difficult times are often more loving, more sharing, more aware of the closeness of God.

Some time ago I talked to Les and Jimmy and Morag. They were shepherding folk in the Scottish Border hills from the 1940s through to the 1970s. They knew difficult, more basic times and, even in retirement, they lived frugally.

I wanted to talk to them about shepherding, but was amazed how often, and how naturally, God came into almost every story.

Morag, Jimmy's wife, stood by the side of his high-backed armchair for almost the entire time we spoke. When she wasn't standing, this eighty-four-year-old woman would rest lightly on the arm of the chair, as if she couldn't bring herself to be too far from her husband.

She recalled times in the winter when her father would take his flock – or hirsel – south to escape the worst of the weather. Young Morag stayed in the family cottage with her brother, her mother, and a baby on the way.

"We sang a lot of hymns to pass dark nights, and they ▶

iStock.

---

by David McLaughlan.

142

were a great comfort," she told me. "There was a stream outside the house for water, although we often had to break the ice. God always provided.

"After two months away, we would look for Dad coming over the hill. If he was on a horse and he was sitting over its hind-quarters, we knew God had provided abundantly.

"You see, the place where the saddle ought to have been would be draped with sacks of flour and the likes. Many a time those sacks were made into clothes or pillowcases."

Jimmy, who had difficulty walking, spent his time carving beautifully intricate walking-stick handles from rams' horns. He recalled a time a flock had been lost in a storm.

Jimmy took Bracken, his collie, and went off in search. Despite knowing the land better than most, he was soon disorientated, soaked, and frozen. When he stumbled into a hole he had fallen into half an hour before, he had to accept that he was completely lost.

"I said, 'Thy will be done, Lord.' Then, because I wanted him safe, I shouted, 'Home!' to Bracken. Any other day he would have gone straight there, but this day he didn't. He stopped and waited for me.

"From somewhere, I was given the strength to climb out of that hole. Bracken walked and stopped, walked and stopped . . . I couldn't imagine he knew where he was going.

"He spent all his time looking back at me. But he took me to the flock, then he took us all home."

He showed me a painting he had done of a storm. There was a sheepdog, looking back, and a small bedraggled shepherd, down on one knee. Behind them both was Jesus, with one hand pointing and the other to his mouth as if he was whistling. The dog was looking at Jesus.

"Maybe it wasn't anything like that," I ventured. "Maybe Bracken just loved you."

"Ach." Jimmy shrugged. "God is love."

I met Les in a nursing home, and his various ailments made him a little short with my sillier question. I got the impression of a rough man who had lived a rough life, even in his prime.

He was disparaging about modern shepherds, with their all-terrain vehicles, and couldn't understand how they got to know their sheep properly like that.

"Breathable" waterproof outdoor clothing was something he respected in theory but had never tried.

"If the weather got really bad," he said, "we just turned our collars up and pulled our caps down."

If ever he had to stay out on the hill overnight, well . . . he only usually

did that if a sheep was ill, in which case he would sit close beside her, each offering a little shelter for the other.

"It must have made for a long night," I said.

"Ach," he replied. "It's a poor man who can't be alone with his thoughts for a while. And then I'd be quiet and listen while the Lord did the talking."

On a bleak hilltop, in the wee small hours, with no other distractions, God must have seemed very close indeed.

Now, don't get me wrong. Anyone who knows me knows I like my comforts. But I also like to step outside them every once in a while.

It might mean sitting on that fallen tree in the woods, it might mean being on my knees in the dirt (in the garden), but often it means sitting on this old-but-noble chair, wishing there was a little more stuffing in the seat.

If we really are closer to God in tough times, then we should appreciate the good times while also understanding that they can be times of less reliance and, thus, more distance.

Les, Jimmy and Morag had dependency woven into the fabric of their lives. We undoubtedly have it much easier these days. For that, we should be thankful, while making sure we are not distracted from our most important relationship.

God of the hard times, be with us also when we are sitting comfortably. ■

Nature's Calendar For *Winter*

Turnips will be at their best now. Substitute them for potatoes in a gratin dauphinoise recipe for a delicious vegetable side dish.

On December 23 in Oaxaca, Mexico, the Noche de Rabanos celebrates the humble radish. Lasting just a few hours, the festival's main spectacle is a huge number of sculptures made out of radishes, often with a seasonally festive theme.

Just like birds, some fish migrate in winter, heading for warmer waters. Although many species of whales do this, the longest migration yet recorded for a fish was a tagged blue marlin which travelled 9,254 miles (14,893 km).

The British winter sun isn't strong enough to help our bodies create vitamin D, so keep your levels topped up by eating foods like fatty fish (tuna and mackerel), eggs, cheese and anything fortified with the vitamin.

"Winter is the time for comfort, for good food and warmth, for the touch of a friendly hand and for a talk beside the fire: it is time for home."
– *Edith Sitwell*

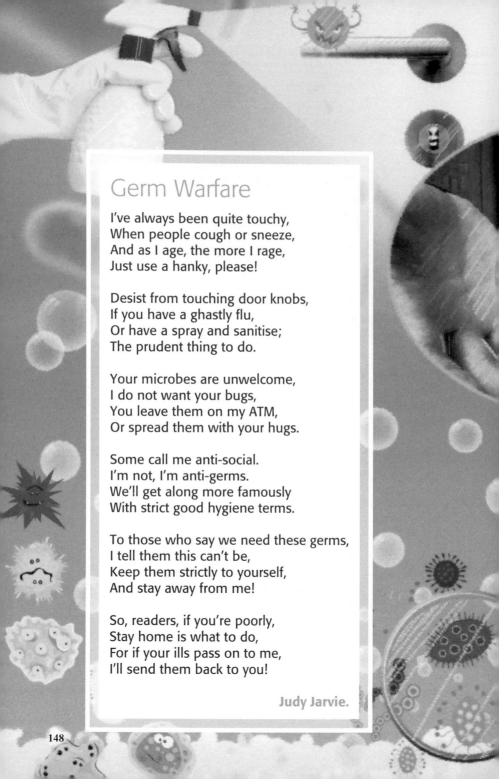

Germ Warfare

I've always been quite touchy,
When people cough or sneeze,
And as I age, the more I rage,
Just use a hanky, please!

Desist from touching door knobs,
If you have a ghastly flu,
Or have a spray and sanitise;
The prudent thing to do.

Your microbes are unwelcome,
I do not want your bugs,
You leave them on my ATM,
Or spread them with your hugs.

Some call me anti-social.
I'm not, I'm anti-germs.
We'll get along more famously
With strict good hygiene terms.

To those who say we need these germs,
I tell them this can't be,
Keep them strictly to yourself,
And stay away from me!

So, readers, if you're poorly,
Stay home is what to do,
For if your ills pass on to me,
I'll send them back to you!

Judy Jarvie.

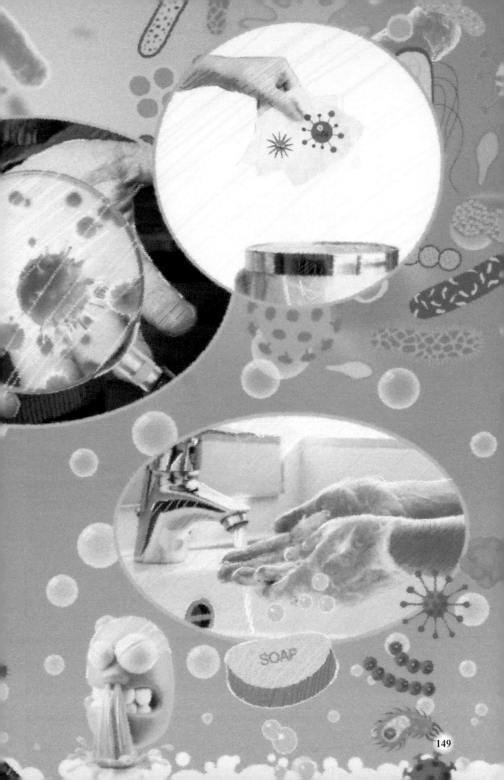

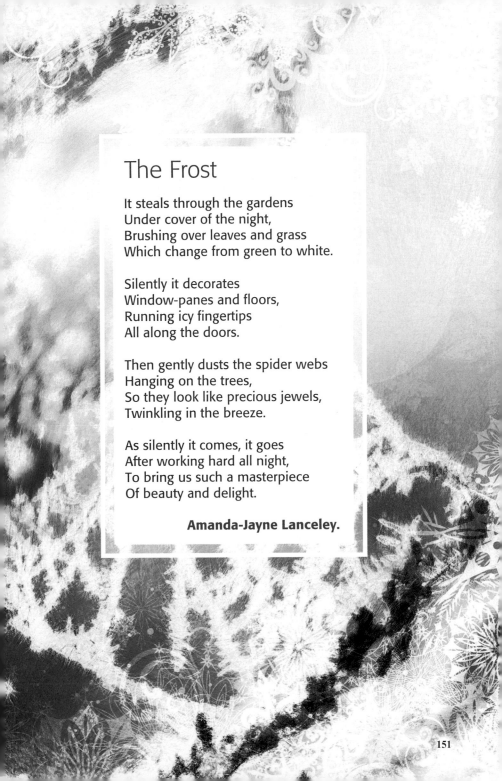

The Frost

It steals through the gardens
Under cover of the night,
Brushing over leaves and grass
Which change from green to white.

Silently it decorates
Window-panes and floors,
Running icy fingertips
All along the doors.

Then gently dusts the spider webs
Hanging on the trees,
So they look like precious jewels,
Twinkling in the breeze.

As silently it comes, it goes
After working hard all night,
To bring us such a masterpiece
Of beauty and delight.

Amanda-Jayne Lanceley.

Old Letters

How precious are those letters that bring to mind a face
Almost lost from memory, and vanished without trace.
A collection of memories that echo through the years;
A certain smile; a well-loved voice that once again one hears.

Someone might keep an album and send them all to you:
Postcards with those souvenirs of things you loved and knew;
They might have lain within a drawer or on some dusty shelf
But suddenly you're face to face with words you wrote
  yourself.

A diary, full of things you did when you were still at school,
That now might make you squirm a bit and think – "Oh, what
  a fool!"
But letters now are e-mails and a text just disappears;
It takes time to write a letter, but it can last for years!

Dawn Lawrence.

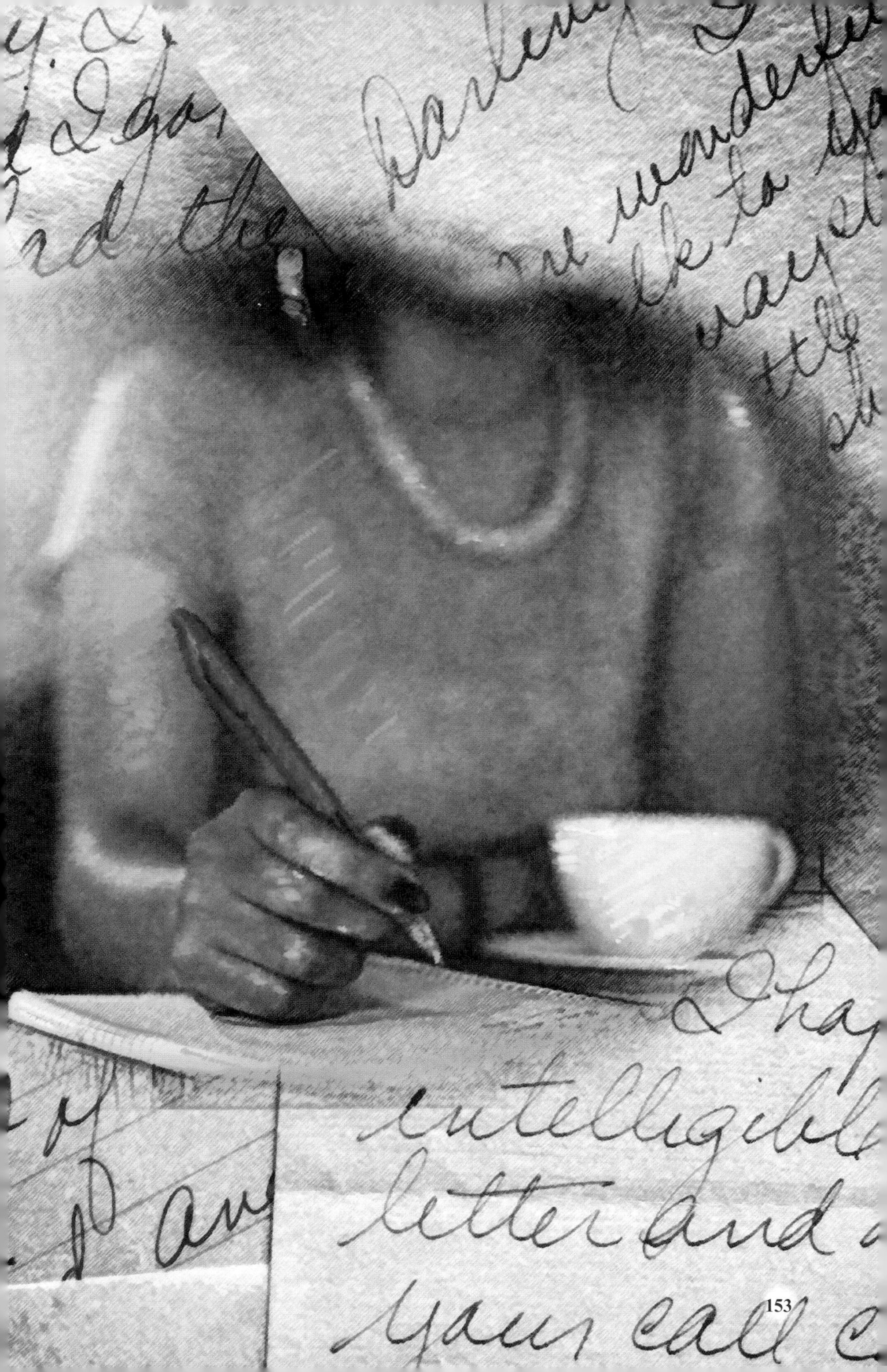

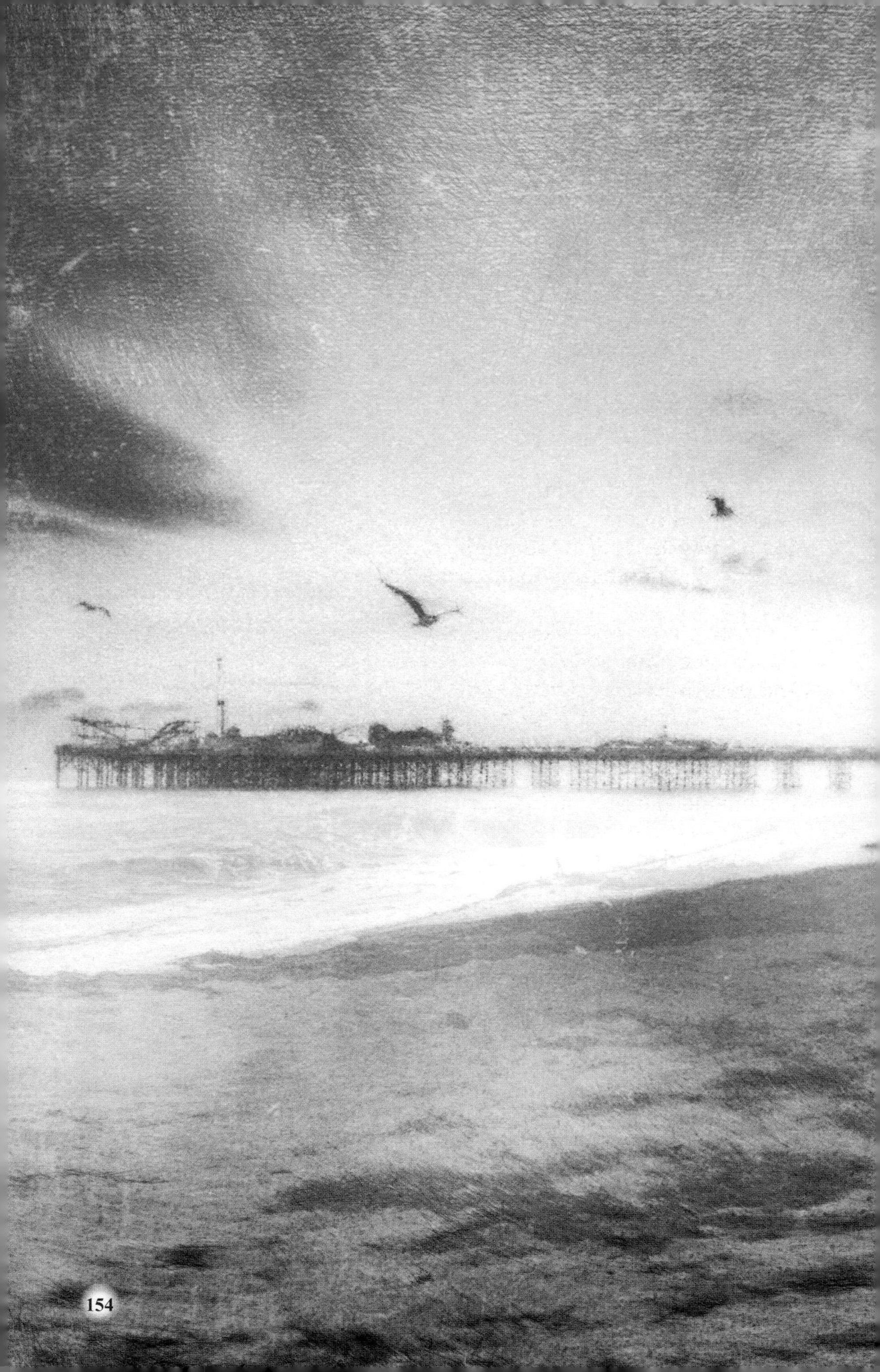

The Pier In Winter

A lively pier in summer sun
Is such a timeless, happy place,
But never so evocative
As when it wears its winter face.

When it's deserted, shuttered down,
It has a magic of its own –
Old posters flapping in the wind
(A wind that numbs you to the bone!)

No colours now, just cold slate grey
That blends both land and choppy sea,
And gulls, no longer summer fed
Soar, keening, skywards, wild and free.

A ghost town, quite devoid of life,
The boarded kiosks, empty strand,
A mist creeps from the sea to chill
The seaweed rotting on the sand.

I guess the reason I enjoy
The pier when it is drab and bare
Is knowing that colour will return
When sun and laughter fill the air!

Eileen Hay.

Heaven On Earth

Suddenly it's snowing
Pure heaven, tumbling down,
Wonderful, white snowflakes
Display a brilliant gown.

Snow gems glitter gloriously
In the shards of sun,
Spilling diamond magic
On freezing vistas spun.

To step on through the glacial charm
That chill upon the cheek.
The robin sports his own design,
Bright red on winter's peak.

Cobwebs silvered on the gate,
Pearl snowdrops in the lane,
This spellbinding scenery
Is heaven on Earth again.

Dorothy McGregor.

Christmas Card Delight

I do love opening Christmas cards,
What picture will I see?
The baby Jesus sleeping
Or a stunning Christmas tree?
A fat and happy snowman,
Or carollers in a park?
One thing I know for sure is that
They're all sent from the heart.

Lily Christie.

We Wish you
a
Merry

To A Candle

From a tiny spark you waken,
Red your core that turns to gold;
Growing in the air that feeds you
Eager; trembling; greedy; bold;
Lighting up the empty darkness,
Twisting, twirling to and fro,
Like a dancer pirouetting,
Shivering slightly as you grow.

What excitement – what a flurry,
Chasing shadows over walls;
Lighting up the hidden corners
Where your warming radiance falls;

I have watched you falter, flutter,
With the merest breath that blows,
But the spark that's lit within you
Simply strengthens, grows and grows.
A sudden light to pierce the darkness,
All those phantoms once so feared,
Fade, like encroaching shadows,
And in your light have disappeared.

Dawn Lawrence.

Amazing Journeys

SOME time around September, there is a great exodus from our shores. I don't mean the hundreds of people leaving on last-minute holiday deals, but the more than one million swallows that leave the safety of their mud and grass nests all across the UK on their migration.

The early broods of youngsters go first, embarking on a journey that involves 200 days of straight flying. A few stragglers may hang around until early October.

The male birds will have been the first to arrive on our shores in their thousands from early April. It's always a treat to see the first swallow. They tell us that summer is on its way.

Many will return to the very nest they had occupied last year, perhaps in a barn or stable, close to large animals like cows and horses which attract the flies that are an easy source of food.

You may have enjoyed watching them this summer, flying low over the fields and meadows, darting this way and that, looping the loop, their dark metallic blue plumage glistening in the sun.

They are experts at catching insects on the wing. The swallows may well have produced two broods over the summer months, and the baby ones would have been spending the warm days improving their flying skills.

Come September, many are to be seen flocking on telephone wires, family upon family of them getting ready to leave. Then one morning they will be gone. No fanfare, no fuss, no last-minute longing look at their summer home.

One hundred years ago, people assumed that birds migrated to warmer lands in the winter, but no-one knew where they went.

No-one ever dreamed it possible that a bird a mere six inches long might fly 6,000 miles to South Africa and back every year.

It was in May 1911 that a lawyer and keen ornithologist, John Masefield, slipped a little ring on to a swallow chick nesting in the porch of his home in ▶

iStock.

by *Janice Ross.*

▶ Cheadle, Staffordshire.

The ring was numbered B830. Can you imagine John Masefield's astonishment when eighteen months later he received a letter telling him that his swallow, B830, had been found in a farmhouse 18 miles from Utrecht, South Africa? This little chick had flown 6,000 miles!

Many people who take late summer holidays to the Mediterranean, especially areas like southern Spain or north Africa, may see these birds as they start their migration.

The swallows fly in a straight line, closely following the Greenwich Meridian Line. How do they know that the shortest distance between two points is a straight line?

Their route goes through France, Spain, Algeria, Mali, Burkina Faso, Ghana and then Togo. Then they turn slightly eastwards and fly to South Africa. It's as well they don't require passports!

The journey will take about twelve weeks. They will fly only during daylight hours, and will cover about 200 miles a day, at an average speed of 20 mph. One was even recorded speeding at 35 mph!

In the early stages they are fit and energetic, and food and water are usually plentiful. The birds will skim across the surface of lakes and rivers, scooping up water and insects as they go.

But we only need to take a look at a map of their travels to see that once they reach the shores of Africa then the journey becomes more hazardous.

Ahead of them will be strong winds and sandstorms threatening to disorientate them, alongside a lack of water and plenty of eagle-eyed predators eager to pick off the weak and flailing.

The birds run the risk of starvation and exhaustion. It has been noted that changes in climatic conditions both across Africa and Europe have meant that many have been returning to their breeding places in a poorer condition, and have been laying fewer eggs.

However, we will no doubt have the joy of seeing these plucky little birds right back at the same nest as last year, ready to start the business of bringing a new family into the world once again.

Amazing as their journey might be, there is an even more amazing journey – one that we will celebrate with the beginning of the season of Advent.

Advent means a coming towards, or an approaching. It heralds the beginning of the Christmas season. Candles will be lit in churches, carols will blare from supermarkets and shopping malls and the pace of life will once again step up a notch.

Advent is really about the approach made by God towards his creation. God wanted to reach the people on Earth with the story of his love.

This involved an amazing journey between Heaven and Earth. It meant God sending his son a long way on a mission to redeem us, starting with being born as a baby in a stable in Bethlehem.

The plan was that Jesus would make his home in our world, bringing the message of God's love and offer of forgiveness to all he encountered.

Like the swallows, there would be many hazards and dangers threatening his very existence.

He would be hunted down as as an infant by a mad king, necessitating that his family become refugees.

He would be tempted cruelly to reveal his power, but would choose resolutely to face the frailty of human flesh. He would be harassed, misunderstood, lied about, mocked, hated and finally crucified.

His death, offered as a substitute for our sin, opened up the possibility for each of us one day to make that journey from Earth to heaven. Now that will be what I call the most amazing of journeys. ∎

Nature's Calendar For *Winter*

Horseradish is easy to grow. This distant relative of cabbage is commonly harvested in winter, and is resilient to harsh weather – it can even survive temperatures of -28 deg. C. (-18 deg. F.)

"Cat Ice" occurs when ice forms on top of water in a thin layer and the water recedes slowly, leaving behind intricate, contour-like patterns. It is so called because the ice is so fragile that it could only support a light-footed cat!

Ptarmigans turn totally white in winter – extremely useful camouflage in the mountains. In the early 1900s, prospectors wanted to name their town in Alaska after the bird. When the spelling proved difficult, they settled for "Chicken" instead!

In 1890, London saw no sunlight for the whole month of December, with a permanently cloudy sky. At the end of that winter in March there would be snow drifts of up to 3.3 metres (11 feet) in the middle of the city.

"I wonder if the snow loves the trees and fields that it kisses them so gently? And then it covers them up snug, you know, with a white quilt; and perhaps it says, 'Go to sleep, darlings, till the summer comes again'." – *Lewis Carroll*

Bing

Old gramophone crackles and pierces
'78s with a needle of steel.
Voice from a box, disembodied,
Floats, hollow and somehow unreal.

Fingers of cloud drifting, ghostly
Across the moon in the crisp air.
Winter solstice cloaks the land early –
This is the darkest time of year.

Beech logs are blazing, flames leaping,
Scents of pine and satsumas ripe
Enrich the room, while on the spruce tree
The pretty lights keep out the night.

An excited child's caught in the magic
Of a distant voice she's always known,
Across the years – telling of children,
Treetops and sleighbells in the snow.

Rebecca Holmes.

Festive Feast

A feast for the senses, is Christmas,
A feast for us all, young and old,
From gingerbread, warm from the oven,
To noses turned pink from the cold.

The sight of green leaves and bright berries,
The mug of hot chocolate that cheers,
They're all part and parcel of Christmas
That stay with us all through the years.

The music that floats from shop doorways,
Old favourites, so corny, yet fun.
The carols piped high by small children,
The magic, for them, just begun.

The resinous tang of the fir-tree,
Its branches a-twinkle with light,
The sparkle of frosty white woodlands,
The hush of a silver-starred night.

So many delights and sensations,
That custom and time cannot pall,
Remind us of blessings abundant
That make Christmas special for all.

Maggie Ingall.

The Star

A hopeful message of God's love
Broke through the darkness, from above,
A story of shepherds tending their sheep,
Excited angels who kept them from sleep.

Choirs sing timeless chants and tunes
While church sills brim with scarlet blooms,
And candles flicker, dispersing the night,
Just like that star so fierce and bright.

I love cards falling through my door,
Paper and ribbons that litter the floor,
Fairy lights sparkle like precious stones,
The story of three kings who left their thrones.

I love cinnamon, truffles and cloves,
The pudding bubbling on the stove,
Yet most of all that star so bright
That goes on glowing, day and night.

Deborah Tomlin.

173

"A single rose can be my garden . . . a single friend, my world."
– Leo Buscaglia